This book belongs
to Cat Lover:

D1636617

What did the feline wear
to the job interview?

A catsuit.

A purring cat is a content cat.

How does a cat like its coffee?

**Heavy milk.
Hold the coffee.**

One cat year equals 15 human years.

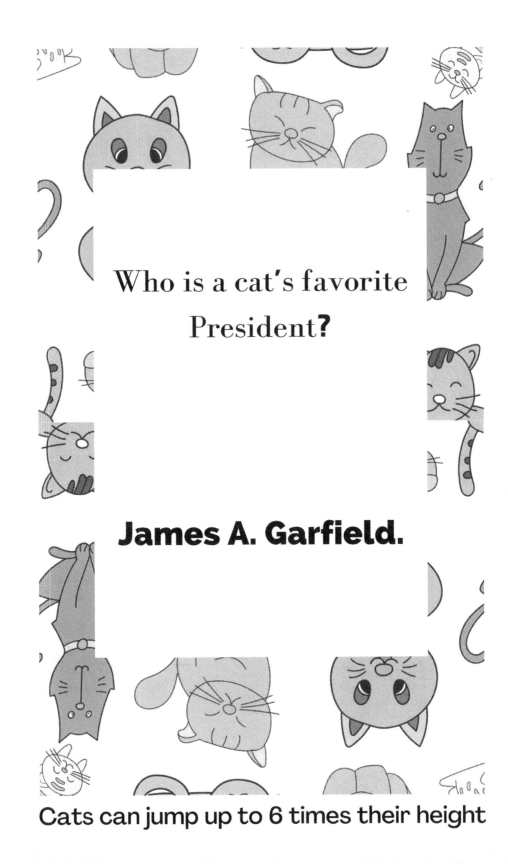

Who is a cat's favorite President?

James A. Garfield.

Cats can jump up to 6 times their height

Why can't the cat ever catch its tail?

It is always behind him.

Cats can't climb with their heads down.

Why did the cat get confused?

They told her to take a liter.

A cat can run up to 30 miles per hour.

What is a cat's favorite television show?

Call Me Kat.

A cat can sleep up to 16 hours per day

Why don't cats like the cartoon Tom and Jerry?

The feel it scripted unrealistic reality television.

Cats have sleeping dreams.

Why was the constrution cat fired from his job?

From all the catcalling he did.

Cats sweat through their paws.

What do you call a supermodel cat?

A glamor puss.

Cats have more bones than humans.

What is a black cat's favorite type of milk?

Chocolate milk.

Cats can jump up to 6 times their height

Do you know cat's are geniuses. I asked my cat, "What is **2** minus **2?**"

My cat looked at me and said nothing.

One cat year equals 15 human years.

Why did the cat take a snoop around the corner?

He was a peeping Tom cat.

A cat can run up to 30 miles per hour.

Why was the cat mad at the Washington D.C. politicans?

Because they have gone to the dogs.

A purring cat is a content cat.

Why don't cats get along with other cats?

They are all too catty.

A cat can sleep up to 16 hours per day

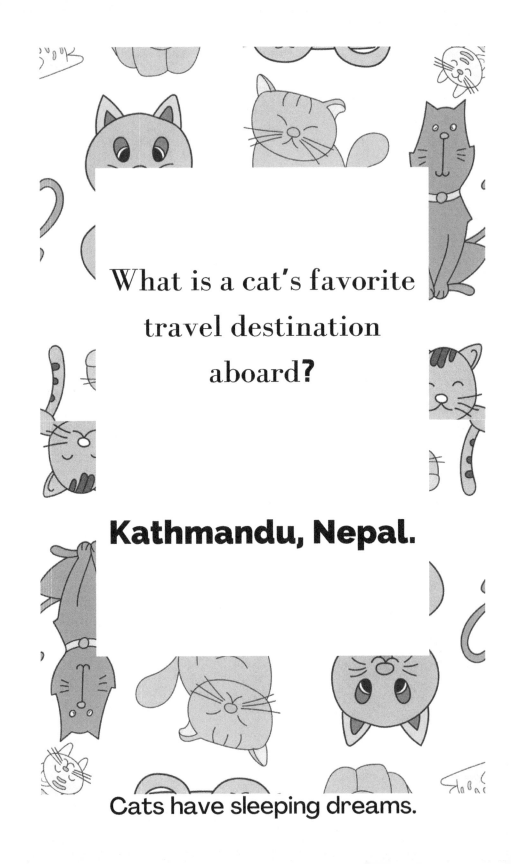

What is a cat's favorite travel destination aboard?

Kathmandu, Nepal.

Cats have sleeping dreams.

What don't you see acts as mascots for firehouses?

They can never find the water hydrants.

Cats can't climb with their heads down.

Two cats go out to dinner on a date, at a fancy restaurant.

The waiter sees them and says, "Sorry, we don't allow pets here."

Cats sweat through their paws.

Whom is the most famous cat?

Cat Stevens.

Cats have more bones than humans.

What do you
call a fat cat?

A portly puss.

Cats have more bones than humans.

What are the cats favorite sports teams?

Detroit Tigers

Cincinatti Bengals

Minnesota Lynx

Jacksonville Jaguars

Carolina Panthers.

What kind of cats love bowling?

Alley cats.

Cats can jump up to 6 times their height

What is the common link between cats and a baseball team on the field?

Nine lives.

A cat can run up to 30 miles per hour.

What is a cat's
favorite car?

A Cat-illac.

One cat year equals 15 human years.

Why are cats good architects?

They can build from scratch.

Cats have more bones than humans.

How did the police identify the cat burglar**?**

Through a fe-line up

A purring cat is a content cat.

How do you know a cat has bad manners?

They never respond to your R.S.V.P.

A cat can sleep up to 16 hours per day

Why did the cat
love yarn?

He was strung out.

Cats have sleeping dreams.

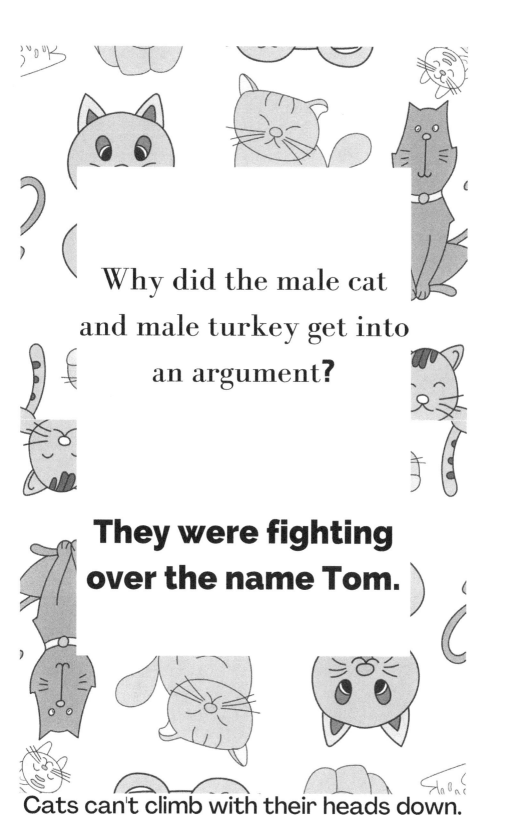

Why did the male cat and male turkey get into an argument?

They were fighting over the name Tom.

Cats can't climb with their heads down.

Why do cats chase mice?

The are hungry.

Cats sweat through their paws.

A dog catcher, dog, cat and mouse walk into a bar.

The bartender goes, "Is this a joke?"

Cats have more bones than humans.

Why do cats eat grass?

They do not like to inhale.

Cats have more bones than humans.

Why do call a cat hooked on catnip?

A feline fanatic.

A cat has 32 muscles in each ear.

What does a cat call its father?

Paw.

Cats can jump up to 6 times their height

What does a cat call its Grandfather?

Paw Paw.

One cat year equals 15 human years.

What is a cat's favorite song?

Black Magic Woman.

Cats can jump up to 6 times their height

What is a cat's favorite condiment?

Cat-sup.

A cat can run up to 30 miles per hour.

Why was the cat fired from the job?

he was cat napping at work.

A cat can sleep up to 16 hours per day

A panther told me he is the richest cat in the world.

Turns out he was lion.

A purring cat is a content cat.

How do cats freshen
their breaths?

They take cat mints.

Cats have sleeping dreams.

What do cats call their owners?

Meow.

Cats can't climb with their heads down.

Why did the boyfriend cat break up with his girlfiend cat?

She was too kneady.

Cats sweat through their paws.

Why did the boyfriend cat break up with his girlfriend cat?

She was too kneady.

Cats have more bones than humans.

What does a cat say after making a joke**?**

Just kitten.

A cat has 32 muscles in each ear.

Why don't you want to play games with a cat**?**

They tend to be cheetahs.

Cats can jump up to 6 times their height

Why aren't cats good story tellers?

They have long tails.

One cat year equals 15 human years.

Why was the animal lover so untrustworthy?

She kept letting the cat out of the bag.

A cat can run up to 30 miles per hour.

What do you call a rude cat?

A curt kitten.

A purring cat is a content cat.

What do you cal a cautious cat?

A pussy footer.

A cat can sleep up to 16 hours per day

What does a cat and mail have in common?

They both go in a box.

Cats have sleeping dreams.

What do you call a dirty cat?

A muddy moggie.

Cats can't climb with their heads down.

What is a cat's nightmare?

To be stranded at a dog show.

Cats sweat through their paws.

How is a cat like a newborn baby?

All they do is eat, sleep and poop.

Cats have more bones than humans.

Wher do cats go to see pin-ups and centerfolds of cats?

Cat fancy.

A cat has 32 muscles in each ear.

What do cats and Santa's reindeer have in common?

They do their best work while you are sleeping.

Cats can jump up to 6 times their height

Why don't cats make good support animals**?**

Cats really don't care.

One cat year equals 15 human years.

Why don't owners, take their cats out for jogging, like dogs?

Cats will leave the house when ready.

A cat can run up to 30 miles per hour.

Why aren't pilots and surgeons good professions for cats?

They tend to fall asleep on the job.

A purring cat is a content cat.

Why was the cat
meowing loudly at night?

**Its a Cat. That is
what they do.**

A cat can sleep up to 16 hours per day

Why are cats good cooks?

They make everything from scratch.

Cats have sleeping dreams.

Why do cats make great golfers?

They are mostly scratch players.

Cats can't climb with their heads down.

Why do cats eat grass?

They do not like smoking it.

Cats sweat through their paws.

Why was the cat such a good motivational speaker?

He always landed on his feet.

Cats can jump up to 6 times their height

Why was the cat such a good motivational speaker?

They can see the light through darkness.

One cat year equals 15 human years.

If, the goat Michael Jordan and a cat got into a jumping contest. Who would win?

The cat. Michael Jordan is the goat.

A cat can run up to 30 miles per hour.

Why can't a cat wear pigtails hair style?

A cat only has one tail.

A purring cat is a content cat.

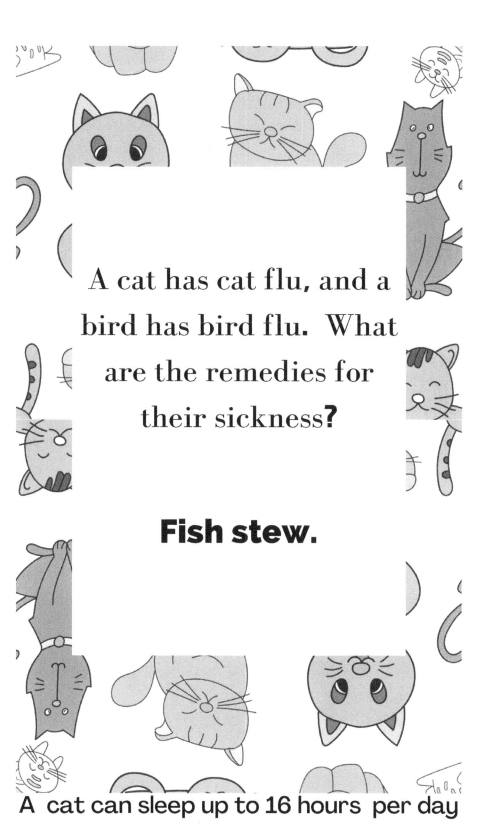

A cat has cat flu, and a bird has bird flu. What are the remedies for their sickness?

Fish stew.

A cat can sleep up to 16 hours per day

A cat, frog, bunny and a squirrel get into a jumping contest. The squirrel wins.

Everybody goes nuts.

Cats have sleeping dreams.

Why don't cats make good drives**?**

Their paws never touch the pedals.

Cats can't climb with their heads down.

What do you
call a fat cat?

A tubby tabby.

Cats sweat through their paws.

What do you
call a fat cat?

A massive mouser.

A cat has 32 muscles in each ear.

What is a cat's favorite song?

What's new Pussycat.

A cat can run up to 30 miles per hour.

What is a cat's favorite movie?

That darn cat.

A purring cat is a content cat.

What is a cat's favorite book?

The Cat in the Hat.

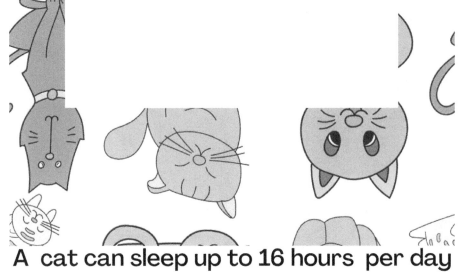

A cat can sleep up to 16 hours per day

What is a cat's least favorite television show?

Dog the Bounty Hunter.

Cats have sleeping dreams.

What do you call several cats sitting on top of each other?

A caterpillar.

Cats can't climb with their heads down.

Why did the cat attack the flower in the garden?

It was a wild cat.

Cats sweat through their paws.

What's a cat's favorite color?

Purrrple.

Cats have more bones than humans.

Why did the **2** big cats get a divorce**?**

One was lion and the other a cheetah.

A cat has 32 muscles in each ear.

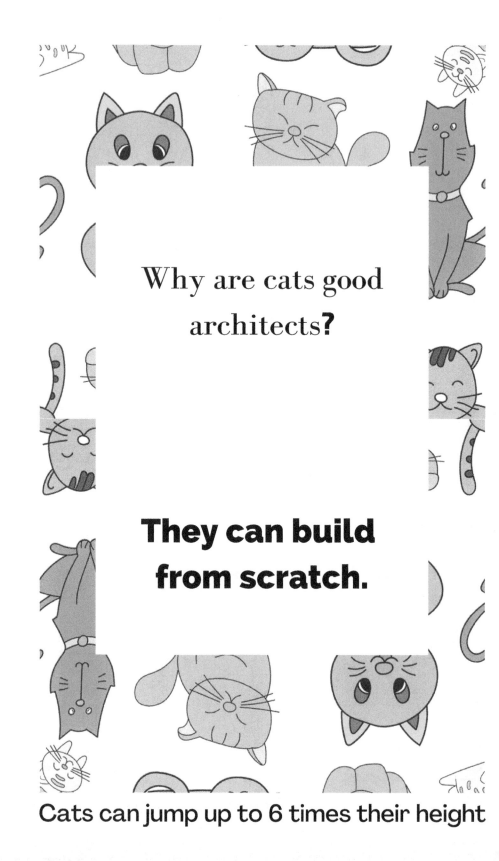

Why are cats good architects?

They can build from scratch.

Cats can jump up to 6 times their height

Why did the fat cat stop drinking milk?

He was on a non-dairy diet.

One cat year equals 15 human years.

A cat and a ghost go out for a drink of milk. The cat gets regular milk. The ghost gets evaporated milk.

A cat can run up to 30 miles per hour.

What is a cat's least favorite milk?

Pea Milk.

A purring cat is a content cat.

Why are cats smarter than dogs?

You will never see cats pulling a sled in Alaska.

A cat can sleep up to 16 hours per day

Why are cats smarter than dogs?

Dogs have blue collar jobs. Cats have glamor jobs.

Cats have sleeping dreams.

Why are cats good landscapers?

They have good lawn-meowers.

Cats can't climb with their heads down.

Why couldn't the cat get the Mona Lisa painting out of the museum?

The red lasers kept him running in circles.

Cats sweat through their paws.

Why do cats leave when you fart?

It smells.

A cat has 32 muscles in each ear.

What did Rip Van Winkle name his cat?

He did not have a cat. He slept for 20 years.

Cats can jump up to 6 times their height

Why are cats good DJs?

They are good at scratching records.

A cat can run up to 30 miles per hour.

Why did the cat hang around the computer?

He wanted to meet the mouse.

A purring cat is a content cat.

How did the cat win the argument?

He had their tongue.

A cat can sleep up to 16 hours per day

How do you know a cat
has bad manners?

**They lick their paws
after eating.**

Cats have sleeping dreams.

How did the cat feel
about the kitty jar?

**He did not like it. It
was to small inside.**

Cats sweat through their paws.

Why are cats good at
video games?

They have nine lives.

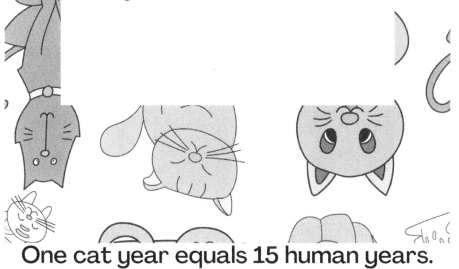

One cat year equals 15 human years.

Why do cats love weddings?

They are good groom-ers.

Cats have more bones than humans.

Why don't cats like the cartoon Tom and Jerry?

Cats feel the characters are unrealistic.

Cats can't climb with their heads down.

Why do cats eat grass?

In the future, they want to run for office.

A cat has 32 muscles in each ear.

What is a cat's favorite song?

Cats in the Cradle.

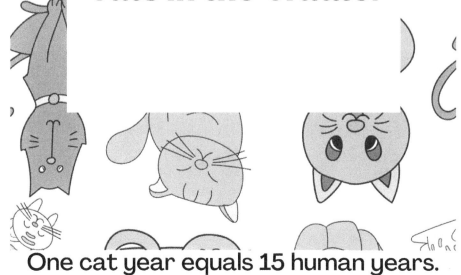

One cat year equals 15 human years.

Why did the cat get annoyed?

He had nothing to ride. The Roomba broke.

A cat has 32 muscles in each ear.

Made in United States
Orlando, FL
07 December 2022

25726617R00055